Adjusting to Life After Loss

Coping with the Death of a Loved One and Honoring Their Memory

Lora C Mercado

Front cover photo © Can Stock Photo / johannesk

Author photo © Joe Ciarrocchi

Marguerite Publishing

http://www.margueritepublishing.com

ISBN: 0692309713
ISBN-13: 978-0692309711

This book and the poem below are dedicated to my precious son, Alex. I love you with every ounce of my soul, sweet baby boy.

<u>White Feathers</u>

Appearing at random
At just the right time
I know it is you
Giving me a gift
My son from heaven
My little angel
A piece of your wing
To give me strength
To live my life
Without you

~ by Lora C Mercado

Introduction

After losing a loved one, we all find ourselves in a state of grief that can go from mild to severe, depending on the situation and how close you were with the one you have lost. After losing my son in 2003, I have experienced many phases of grief and healing. My goal in writing this book, is to help bring peace and comfort to those who are finding it hard to cope with the reality of their new life, without the one that has passed away.

I hope that this book will bring a new sense of calm and happiness back into your life.

~ Lora C Mercado

Chapter 1:

Getting Through the Grief

I am a mother who has lost a child. I am a daughter who has lost a father. I am a granddaughter who has lost each of her grandparents. I have lost numerous friends. I have lost furry friends too. Grief is familiar to me.

Over the years, through each of my losses, I have grieved differently. The pain was deeper with some than with others. I still struggle with the loss of my son, and I miss being able to talk to my father. I wish my grandparents could have met my beautiful daughter, and see how much I have matured over the years. I long to snuggle with my cats that have passed away throughout my life.

Eventually, we are all faced with the death of someone that we love. Along with the absence of their presence, comes the overwhelming emotions of grief. But we're usually ill prepared, because death is often sudden.

Conflicting emotions of sorrow, anger, loneliness,

sadness, shame, anxiety and guilt may accompany grief, making it all the more stressful. Failing to work through each stage of grief means it takes longer for healing to occur. Although this can be a painful process, it's important to deal with your feelings because it affects your future emotional and physical well-being.

To grieve the death of a loved one may seem unbearable, but it's actually healing. Mourning is different for each person and below are some steps to help you through the grieving process.

1. Accept your loss.

It may be tempting to deny the loss of a loved one by acting as if it's not a big deal or pretending they've gone away. But preferably sooner rather than later, you need to accept the person has gone and won't be coming back.

2. Focus on getting through one hour at a time.

At first your loss will feel horrific, and surviving without your loved one seems impossible. You lack the will to do anything. Things you used to do automatically are now difficult. By living one hour at a time, you will feel reassured when you're able to do even mundane tasks, like getting out of bed in the morning, dressing yourself, eating food or taking a bath.

3. Live one day at a time.

When you realize you'll survive your loss, albeit reluctantly, live one day at a time. Soak up the sympathy you receive from family, friends and members of your community. The knowledge that you have the support of a close circle of family and friends will go a long way to helping with your recovery.

You'll also need time alone to fall apart, to feel your pain without worrying about taking care of others. It's unhealthy to hold in so much emotion, and others will feel uncomfortable if they see you at your most distraught.

4. Look after yourself.

Throwing yourself into your work, sleep, exercise, food or alcohol prolongs the grieving process. Instead, develop a routine. Familiar tasks which require little thought provide a comforting structure around which you can base your day.

Eat nutritious food, and if you aren't hungry take a multi-vitamin or drink a meal replacement shake. Bath or shower once a day.

Dealing with death is exhausting and stressful.

You'll find yourself emotionally and physically depleted, so rest often. Get lots of sleep and don't overtax yourself. Structure with regard to self-care habits is one way to help you as you come to terms with your loss.

When you feel like you're losing it, do something purely for yourself. Run, meditate, hit a punching bag, scream, pray, go for a drive. Do whatever you need to do, in order to cope with the grief, without feeling guilty about it.

Expect to cry often, you may even cry in public. It's a normal part of the grieving process so don't be embarrassed. Crying is cathartic.

5. Have faith.
People who believe in God or a higher power tend to cope better. Being grateful for your blessings, and prayers of thanks in good times, is just as important as praying when you're in trouble. If you're spiritual, praying and meditation can give you much needed strength.

Chapter 2:
Stages of Grief

There are many out there that don't know the difference between bereavement and grief. Bereavement is simply the general process of recuperating after the passing of a loved one. Grief is the individual reaction to this process. Grief can come in many forms including depression, anger, regret, loneliness, or even sometimes relief. None of these emotions are wrong, what's important is how the person lives through them.

The Seven Stages of Grief:

It's generally believed that these are the most common stages of grief but they may vary from person to person and with the circumstances involved.

1. Shock - Upon first hearing the news, it is common for the individual to not react at all or to be in a literal state of shock. This allows the person the necessary time to process the information.

2. Denial - The initial reaction once everything begins to sink in is to pretend like nothing happened. It's an escape mechanism that, again, allows the person more time to recover. An individual in this stage should not be confronted.

They will come through in their own time.

3. Anger - Through the shock and denial stages, emotions have been building up so it is not uncommon for the bereaved person to release these emotions in a fit of anger. This anger can be falsely directed at anyone or anything so it is best to stay neutral without abandoning them.

4. Depression - This stage is when everything truly sinks in. It may be triggered by the person recalling a fond memory or performing some action as if the deceased were still alive and with them. Thought patterns and actions can become irrational during this time so it is best to stay close. Do not try to talk the person out of anything, instead provide comfort.

5. Pain and Guilt - It is not uncommon for the person to feel guilty for the loss and experience intense pain because of it. Do not mask this pain or cover it up with alcohol or drugs.

6. Testing and Reconstruction - As the person begins to work through their emotions and accept reality, they will begin to turn to realistic and truly helpful solutions.

7. **Acceptance** - Finally embracing the situation and moving forward with your life. This

stage does not ensure happiness or that the person will go back to their normal life. By now they are in a state well enough to enjoy their life again, and come to terms with everything that has happened.

Recovering from Grief:

Everybody deals with things in their own way and in their own time. Do not rush this process in any way. Understand that grief is not always a one time thing. It can return with a vengeance at any time.

If you continue to severely struggle for a long period to time, it is advised to consult a licensed and qualified mental health professional.

Chapter 3:
Types of Grievers

After our son died, my husband and I dealt with the loss in completely opposite ways. I was paralyzed and cried all the time. He threw himself into his work, and didn't cry as much as I thought he should have. I was making the assumption that his lack of tears was equal to his lack of grief. I couldn't have been more wrong.

At the time, neither of us had ever experienced such a great loss, and we were both doing the best we could with the cards we were dealt. I didn't realize that his pain and grief was just as deep as what I was going through, but he just had to process it in his own way.

Kenneth Doka, who wrote the book "Grieving Beyond Gender", developed the idea of two patterns of grieving: the intuitive pattern and the instrumental pattern. Intuitive grievers express grief in an affective way, which means they adapt to it by showing emotions. Instrumental grievers experience grief physically, such as in a restlessness or by thinking about it on a cognitive level. They adapt to it by thinking it through or wanting to do something actively.

Intuitive Grievers:

· Experience waves of emotions

· Express grief mirroring the inner experience: cry, scream and shout

· Say: "I just feel sad all the time" or "I have this overwhelming sense of sadness."

· Are often disenfranchised later in the process: "What is wrong with this person? Why are they still crying?"

· Helpful for them: therapy, support groups, talking to a trusted friend, journaling or internal process to explore those emotions

Instrumental Grievers:

· Experience in a physical or cognitive way: by continuously thinking about the deceased, running over the things that happened, feeling like they have been punched or kicked in the stomach

· Express grief not consciously, but may talk about the deceased a lot or actively set up a charity

· Say: "I just can't concentrate, I can't focus since he died" or "I cannot stop thinking about her."

· Are often disenfranchised early in the process: "What is wrong with this person? Why isn't he crying? Why are they not just getting over it?"

· Emotional expression is muted

· Helpful for them: the "doing"

These two patterns should not be seen as either/or options, but rather as the two ends of a continuum with various blended options in between. Generally speaking, women often process grief in the intuitive style, where men more often are instrumental grievers. This can often lead to misunderstandings in the relationship. It is however, important to note, that neither of those patterns is better than the other, it is just one of the many ways to experience and express grief.

Blended patterns are a mixture of both intuitive and instrumental reactions, and responses to mourning. According to Doka and Martin's book, "Grieving Beyond Gender: Understanding the Ways Men and Women Mourn", there are also those individuals who show inconsistencies between the ways that grief is experienced and expressed, which is called dissonant.

When dealing with grief as a couple it is important to accept and understand each other's different strategies and allow room for the individual's personal experience.

Chapter 4:
Grieving the Loss of a Child

My first born child, Alexander was born with a serious and rare congenital heart defect in 2002. We found out about his defect when he was five days old, and that there was a strong chance that he may not survive. I will never forget looking into the doctor's face as he told me those words. I can still see everything like it was yesterday. It was so surreal. One day we were happy, brand new parents, the next day we found out there were some health issues and not to worry, then the following day we found out that our son may die.

I felt as though my world was ripped out from under me. My beautiful baby was being poked and prodded and needed extensive heart surgery that was not guaranteed to work. I remember wishing that I could put him back inside my womb where he was safe, but that was not reality. He needed to undergo the heart surgery to have any chance of survival, so we went through with it, hoping for the best.

Ultimately, my son passed away in my arms at 22 days old. I remember holding him in my arms and feeling the emptiness of his body after his last breath. I held him for hours after he passed away. I would put his tiny little blanket wrapped body onto the bed, kiss him and try to walk out of the room. This happened so many times, because I just couldn't leave him there, all alone, so tiny and so precious. I just wanted to wake up from this nightmare. Eventually, I had to let him go. I stared at his hospital window from the parking lot on that cold January night. I just couldn't believe my beautiful son was gone forever...

The days following his passing were a blur. We had to plan his funeral and try to process what just happened. Time continued on and the phone calls from concerned friends stopped. It felt like they were afraid to talk to me and didn't know how to handle my sadness. It is common for friends to shy away after a death, but showing support is always a better choice. I had to find a way to cope with my loss on my own. My husband dealt with things by throwing himself into his work. I, on the other hand, could hardly function for the first few months after Alex passed away.

I decided to try a support group at a local hospital for mothers who are experiencing infant loss. I didn't feel like that was the group for me, so I kept looking for others that may suit me better.

There is a local Compassionate Friends chapter near

me, so my mother and I attended a meeting, not knowing what to expect. I am so thankful for the kindness and empathy that I received from that beautiful group of people who were also struggling with the loss of their child. I finally felt that people understood me and how sad I was. It was ok to cry, and it was ok not to. It was comforting to be able to talk to people who understood all of the emotions and issues I faced as a bereaved parent. I was in a room of acceptance and understanding, and that is when I started to heal.

I attended these meetings for a couple of years after my son's death. Each year, we continue to attend the Worldwide Candle Lighting at the local chapter and also participate in their yearly Walk To Remember, which also includes a beautiful butterfly release. These acts of acknowledgment make it feel that our son is still a part of our lives, and it gives us a chance to focus solely on him, even though his is not here physically.

On my son's birthday, my family writes little notes and we attach them to helium balloons. We sing happy birthday and release them into the sky. We will watch them in silence until we can no longer see them. I always have a little cake with his name on it and we all blow out his candles together. It is emotional, yet cathartic, and I know that he is looking down on us with as much love as we send him from where we are.

Grief in the Family Unit

The loss of a child will impact not only the parents, but also the whole family. Within every family is a balance. The parents have developed their own roles and the children will have their roles in relation to this. There will not only be acute pain and grief, but also a change in the balance of the family. We all express our grief in different ways and at different times. With the loss of a child, a brother, a sister, each family member will express their loss in a unique way at different times. This can cause tensions. Why is one child apparently more or less upset than the other? Parents can be angry that they are not each feeling the same way, or expressing their grief in a similar manner.

If families do not mourn openly, there can be problems expressing the grief, which can cause long term issues. Silence can lead to a downward spiral of grief. The changes that will take place within a family are very difficult to acknowledge, or even assess from within the family, especially if there is this silence. It means you have to be brave to express your grief. In reality, it is sensible to seek some sort of help to deal with the unbearable grief when a child dies.

Be aware that trying to protect your family by being secretive or closed about your grief, is counter-productive and may have bad long-term effects. Children will copy and mimic their parents in the belief that this is the right behavior. In that case, the mourning process can be suppressed. The mourning process and a shared journey of grief, discovering the new identities within the family, is one thing that can really help.

In the developed world, the loss of a child is a rare thing. We are used to children surviving into adulthood, so this type of bereavement can be more difficult to understand than the loss of someone older. As a consequence, it is likely that people will say things to you that you would rather not hear. These things may make you angry. It is fine to be angry if people say stupid things. Most likely they are trying to make you feel better, but are at a loss for the right words, because they have never experiences a similar loss. If there are people that say things that upset you on a constant basis, keep your distance from them until you feel you are strong enough to handle it.

Chapter 5:
Grieving the Loss of a Spouse or Partner

We grieve because we've lost. We grieve because we've loved. We grieve because of endings. We grieve because what we wanted to be "forever" is no longer. Wow, what high expectations we have. We expect to love forever when we take vows of "until death do us part." When what that really implies, is the impermanence of life.

The reality of our marriage vows are merely words spoken on that special day because usually one is not thinking of death, but instead of a happy life together forever. But, what happens when being together is no longer, because death has interrupted it? Is the grief process any different if the couple were married two years or sixty-two years?

I recall a story from years ago, of a lady and her newly married husband, who went on an extravagant honeymoon, following a beautiful wedding. Days later, her husband of just a few days, died while on a tourist outing. She said her forever ended before it even began. She had to return home, all alone, to an empty and newly decorated house, filled with unopened wedding gifts and notes of wedding blessings. Of course, she received many acknowledgments of sympathy from friends, and even those who didn't know her, but were affected by the story. Neighbors near the church, who witnessed the horse and carriage after the wedding ceremony, were in disbelief, as they were still picturing that memorable wedding day.

Was it the death that caused such a shock, the timing of the death, the series of events, the remembrance of the ceremony, or the sorrow felt for the bride? It could have been any of these, but the reality is that her forever, as she had expected it to be, was no longer forever.

Death, no matter what the cause or the situation (lengthy illness, stillborn baby, sudden accident, murder, suicide, etc.) is always unexpected. We are never prepared for our hopes, dreams, and expectations of forever to be shattered. We aren't prepared for our forever to be cut short of our self-imposed timeline. So, what happens when our forever is no longer forever?

We must travel the road of grief. One must take the grief journey because there is no way around it; but, there is hope for getting through it. We are all unique individuals and we each grieve differently. There is no set time frame for grieving; however, doing the grief work can shorten the time that one grieves. It can help with acknowledging and accepting the death and the emotions associated with the loss. Then, it can help one move forward on the journey of rebuilding their new life going forward.

Everything in life is temporary, including life itself. Decide to say yes to the gift of now. Now, this very moment, is all that is guaranteed to you. I encourage you to say yes to this moment and live your life. Yes, cherish the memories of your dear loved one, but also embrace your future. What are you uniquely here on this planet to do now? Who are you to help? What action step can you take today to move forward?

Statistics show that it normally takes 5-8 years to recover from a devastating loss, although I feel that nobody can ever technically "get over it". We learn to cope and live our lives again, slowly but surely.

Dating After the Death of a Spouse or Partner
How long should a widowed person wait before dating? Are you wondering if you are ready to date again? What will be expected of you? Have you asked yourself what your family will think? If you have been married most of your life, and then find yourself single again because of the death of your

spouse, you may be wondering what is appropriate behavior during this time.

The dating scene can be overwhelming in this day and age. The rules may have changed since you dated last, but during this process don't lose yourself. It is important that you learn to like the person that you are single, before being a part of a new relationship.

There are many fears about dating. Often, the best way to start is by attending social events with your date and other people. Enjoying someone's company in an environment that is non-threatening, is a good way to feel at ease at first. If you don't hit it off, it's a lot easier to part ways. Dating is not the same thing as having a relationship, and each date does not have to become serious. People date for different reasons. Some people just want to be in a serious relationship again, yet others enjoy the social aspect, such as someone to go to the museum with, or to attend a Saturday matinee.

When you become more serious about a new person, the question arises as to what your family will say about your choice. Hosting a dinner party is a great way for your friends, and others who care for you, to be introduced to this new person in your life. Keep in mind that these people, though glad that you are socializing again, enjoy your company as an individual as well. Don't get so caught up in the dating, and being with someone every minute, that you forget about the other people in your life. Also, don't feel guilty for dating. Your significant other would want you to live your life, and not stay home alone most of the time.

Dating should be fun, not hard work. You are in a new chapter of your life. Keep in mind that dating doesn't have to lead to a permanent relationship. Finding the right person, after the death of someone you loved dearly, is a challenge. Take your time and enjoy the process.

Chapter 6:
Grieving the Loss of a Parent

I lost my father in 2008 after an illness. Although he had been sick for quite a while, his death was very sudden and took me by surprise. He had suffered a massive stroke while on a ventilator due to pneumonia. He didn't want to live his life incapacitated, so the hospital told us that he needed to be removed from the ventilator that was keeping him alive. My sister and I watched him gasp for air continuously for hours after they took the ventilator off. It was the most excruciating thing to hear that noise. I will never forget it. We pleaded with him to go to the light, and we repeatedly told him how much we loved him. It was awful to see him like that.

The nurses told us it could be days or hours until he finally passed. My sister and I had just traveled ten hours by car to get there, and were physically drained. We decided that we would go to the hotel for a short nap and return in a few hours. I felt guilty, but we were so exhausted, that was the best thing for us to do. Within an hour and a half, the hotel called my cell phone and told us to hurry and get there, because he was passing away right then. Needless to say, we didn't make it in time. I believe he was waiting to be alone so he could die in peace.

I still feel guilty for not being there when he passed, but I guess that is not how it was meant to be. His spirit needed to be alone, which makes me sad.

I will never forget looking at how weak, small, and yet peaceful my father looked after he passed. It was so surreal. He and I had always had strife in our relationship. I loved him, but he never really showed love in return. Now there would never be a chance, and that shook me to the core. It is still very strange to not be able to pick up the phone and hear his voice. It is a void that is virtually indescribable.

The fact is that most of us will eventually experience the loss of a parent. Statistics show that twelve million Americans every year, endure the grief and loss of a parent. No matter how old or young we are, the loss of a parent leaves us feeling orphaned or abandoned, and perhaps even though the death was expected, we are reeling with shock.

It is true that the world is a very different place when we have to live in it without our parents. Beneath every adult facade, there is a small child who still wants a hug and a kiss from mommy, or a joke and a kind word from daddy. These feelings are what sustain our memories, and carrying on loving traditions is a healthy way to grieve as well as grow from this loss.

Death is a lesson in life, and the death of our own parents is an important lesson we learn in respect of our own aging process. It is important to rely on a support system, and teach your own children to do the same. One very important lesson is learning to express the love you have for special people, while still alive. Tomorrow is never promised, and we must keep that in mind when communicating with the ones we love. I never like to leave or hang up the phone without saying, "I love you" to my family.

Nothing is ever the same after the loss of a parent, which essentially means that your family history has changed irrevocably. However, all is not lost, as we also have a wealth of fond memories as well as family traditions. In terms of our life's meaning, these memories are a treasure. Reliving traditions is a way of not only honoring the parent(s), but of bringing a sense of continuum to the nurturing and love, as well as the guidance we received from them. We miss them, so we can comfort ourselves, by maintaining old traditions, and even beginning new rituals. We actually may be burying some of our past with our parent, and writing a new family chapter.

It is comforting to include the memory of a parent who has passed away in a new family ritual. There are many ways to establish new rituals which may become family tradition. It could be as simple as laying an extra place at the table at Thanksgiving or Christmas, or possibly simply lighting a candle in their memory on their birthday. Donate to a charity or give of your time to a pet charity your parent admired. Many wealthy families set up scholarships in the name of their respective parents.

It does not take money however to keep memory alive - a wonderful way to honor a parent is to give back to the community in which they lived and died. Share memories together with other family members and friends, this does not have to be a dour occasion; amusing or enlightening anecdotes have a way of coming out regardless, and humor can be very cathartic.

Creating small rituals is a good way to heal after loss; they assist in establishing spiritual meaning and allow you to respond in a purposeful way to a significant change in your life.

Chapter 7:
Grieving the Loss of a Sibling

<u>Child Siblings:</u>

The death of a loved one is never an easy thing. The death of a sibling is especially difficult for a child. Many times, the parents are so involved with their own grief that others may need to be involved in helping a child through their grief.

Children see the world "in black and white". Depending on the age of the child, and the experiences of their lives, they may have a great deal of difficulty grasping the concept of death. When their sibling dies and they attend the services, they see them as sleeping, and wonder at all of the tearful people in attendance. Even if they have had the benefit of someone trying to explain death before attending, the black and white of the world still says that their sibling is asleep.

They may have some basic questions:
- Why is everyone crying?
- How did my sibling get here?
- Is he coming home with us?
- Why is he sleeping here?
- Why doesn't s/he wake up?

They may be angry or overly upset at the process. If

they know what the traditions are as far as what to expect at the services and the burial, they may decide that they want to attend, or that they can only handle a part of it.

Here are a few pointers to keep in mind:
- It is best to follow their lead concerning allowing them to attend.
- Have a designated person to look after the child since it is likely that the parents will not be able to.
- Expect that they may request to leave at any point. If they do, leave - immediately.
- Try to answer any questions honestly.

The circumstance of the death will play a major role in explaining what has happened to a child. An extended illness is a little easier to explain because it allows plenty of time to talk about the illness and expectations. A sudden, unexpected death leaves children feeling as lost as it does adults, maybe more so. In the case of an illness, it is important to remember that children understand "catching" a cold that their friend or classmate has. The idea of catching an illness that "the doctors can not make better" will occur quickly to them.

Adult Siblings:

People always consider the grieving processes of parents, children, and spouses, but the sibling grieving process can sometimes take a backseat. Still, the loss that you feel when a brother or sister dies, is very real and can be extremely painful. Few people are going to understand you, as well as your sibling did, or the impact that the loss of that companionship will make on your life. Even if you and your sibling did not spend a lot of time together as adults, it will still take an emotional toll on you.

Below are some ideas to help you still feel connected to your sibling, and keep their memory alive:

Do Things They Used to Like

One of the ways that you mat want to reconnect with your sibling after they pass, is to start spending some time doing things that they liked to do. If they enjoyed hiking and fishing, why not do the same as an attempt to reconnect spiritually? If they loved movies, have a marathon where you watch their favorite titles. Find some things that they enjoyed, and experience them for yourself.

Similarly, if you both used to take a few days off every year to go on a road trip together, consider continuing the tradition, rather than letting it languish. You could go on your own, go with another sibling, or friends of your sibling. Do what you can to keep the happy memories flowing. These are the kinds of things your brother or sister would have wanted you to do.

Try to Find a Special Support Group

It may be difficult to find support groups that deal with the topic of sibling loss specifically. Still, it's a good idea to look for a group in your area, such as The Compassionate Friends, who deals with child and sibling loss. If you cannot find one specifically, you may want to see about starting an informal group, where people will be able to get together and discuss what they are feeling, and talk about the various methods they might be using to cope with the loss.

The Silver Lining in the Storm Cloud

The good news is that you are going to be able to get through this difficult time. You are not going to have to deal with the overwhelming amount of pain that you feel right now forever. You can start looking for ways to remember all of the good that your brother or sister brought into your life and the lives of others they touched. Get together with family and friends on their birthday and celebrate the life that they were fortunate enough to have lived. Remember those good times, and use those to color your memories of your sibling, rather than the grief that you are feeling right now. Yes, it is difficult. But the good news is that you really can move on and heal.

Chapter 8:
Grieving the Loss of a Friend

I have lost quite a few friends, some from illness, others from suicide, or other reasons. I coped with each loss differently, depending on how close we were, and what the circumstances were behind their death. Reflecting back on times we shared helped me to get through the grieving period, but the pain was still very strong. There are a few friends that I think of that are no longer alive, and I still well up with tears, even though it has been many years since their passing.

Coping with loss of a friend is never easy, but such losses can be especially trying, because they also force us to come to terms with our own mortality. No matter if your background is religious or otherwise, it's important to allow yourself to go through the process of grieving, which can present itself in different ways for each individual situation.

Steps for Coping with a Friend's Death:

1. Accept that grieving takes time.
Too often, our culture equates "strength" with emotional emptiness or stoicism in the face of

tragedy. In order to properly move through the grieving process and to heal from your loss, you need to allow yourself time to feel your natural emotions. There is no right or wrong way to feel, and there is no set amount of time that you will take to heal. The important thing to remember, is to give yourself time to experience your loss and the emotions that accompany it.

2. Acknowledge the seriousness of your loss.

It's tempting to diminish the importance of your loss by comparing yourself to those who have less (e.g. people living in the third world, people who have lost more loved ones in natural disasters, etc.), but this is not ultimately helpful to the grieving process. You can do the most good for the world when you are fully recovered from your wounds, so allow yourself to feel deeply hurt by a friend's death. Only by acknowledging your pain will you be able to recover from it.

3. Engage in activities you enjoy.

Don't feel as if you need to go through a period of deep mourning that excludes activities you love. Spend time doing things that make you happy, even if they remind you of your friend. Joy is an acceptable (and even desirable) emotion in the healing process. Sometimes you may feel guilty for moments when you find yourself happy. This is a normal process of grieving, but you should allow your happiness to shine through so you can continue living your life to the best of your ability.

4. Reach out to others who are grieving.
In all likelihood, you aren't the only one hurt by your friend's death. Talk with those in your circle who are feeling similar pain, and allow yourselves to remember and honor your friend's life.

5. Accept support from friends and family.
Those who did not know or were not close to your friend can be a great source of strength. Allow others to offer their support, even if it seems as if it will not help. Interaction with loved ones is one of the most powerful medicines available.

6. Channel your emotions.
Try writing your thoughts in a journal, poem, or song; planting a garden or tree in your friend's honor; painting or drawing to illustrate your pain; or otherwise "doing something" with the pain you're feeling. Art is a potent healer. You will be amazed at the release you will feel just by painting abstractly on a canvas. You will notice the colors that you choose will vary upon your mood. When you are feeling anger, you may tend to paint in more red tones, but if you are sad or reflective, your work may have more blue and purple tones.

Creativity is one of the best outlets for releasing pain from grief, or anything else that you may be going through. Once you let your emotions out in a tangible form, they will not weigh you down, as if you kept them bottled up inside.

Chapter 9:
Grieving the Loss of a Pet

Over the years I have had to say goodbye to quite a few of my beloved cats. They lost their battle to illness after providing years of loyalty, amusement, and devotion. My heart broke as I held my faithful companions while they took their last breath. Saying good-bye was our final moment together. I had stayed with them to offer compassion and comfort until the end. What greater love is there, than to put your own feelings aside for the love and well being of another? They passed this life peacefully, while in the arms of love, and that was the best thing I could give to them at that final moment.

My "best friends" were cats, but that in no way diminishes the love I shared, or the pain I felt when letting them go. Two of my cats passed away when I was not with them, and it makes me so sad to know that I wasn't there in their time of need. I would never intentionally leave them at a time when they desperately needed my comfort.

Grieving the loss or death of a pet can be extremely painful. In many cases, a pet has become a friend, a confidant, a buddy, and even a comforter. Pets selflessly give us companionship, faithfulness, acceptance and unconditional love; they enrich our lives without a doubt. Many times, pets are treated as family members and participate in regular household activities and even family outings. They work their way into our daily lives, the family unit, and ultimately into our hearts. Their innocence and carefree attitudes bring a lighter side to life and is a welcome attribute to most homes. Pets offer so much joy with their presence, therefore when they are gone, there's a void. This kind of loss is significant and should be recognized as such.

The pain and sense of loss can be overwhelming. Even though the grief is powerful, it is still experiencing "good grief"; it is an active grief. Acknowledge your feelings openly, and not pressing them down, only to rise up later. Grief of any kind should not be ignored; it must be addressed head on so it can eventually fade. Talk about your feelings, the situation, and let out any emotions to someone trusted. It may also help to talk about the memories and reflect on good times. This can be a painful process, but necessary for progression.

Memorial Ideas:

Urn

There is such a large variety of pet urns available online and also through your veterinarian. Find one that fits the personality of your pet, that you can display in your home. Many decorative urns look like figurines, and nobody would even know that it was actually a cremation urn unless they were told.

Jewelry

Pendants can be made that include a place to put a small amount of your pet's ashes. Some companies will also engrave your pet's paw print or nose print on the pendant. It only requires a high resolution close up photo to be able to produce the print. There is no ink needed. Here is a link to a resource for this type of jewelry: http://www.memorialgallerypets.com/pet-noseprint-pawprint-jewelry.aspx

Garden Memorial Stone

You can purchase beautiful marble or granite stones to place in your flower garden or near your pet's favorite outdoor spot. These can be customized with names and also come ina variety of shapes and sizes. These can be readily found online.

Portrait

Find a local or online artist who can bring your pet's personality to life in a painting or drawing that you can display in your home for years to come.

Photo Book

There are many online services that make it simple to design and print hard cover photo books. Gather all of your favorite photos of you pet, and upload them to create your own personal memory book. This would also make a nice keepsake to give a child or friend who recently lost a pet.

Tattoo

Since the popularity of tattoos has increased over the last few decades, it is common to get a tattoo in memory of your favorite pet. Be sure to check out samples of the artist's work and the cleanliness of the tattoo shop before committing to it. Do not get the tattoo on a whim. Be sure to think about it for a while prior to your appointment.

Chapter 10:
Grief of a Caregiver

Caring for someone who is in poor health, especially when it's a parent, is never an easy undertaking. The burdens are made heavier, by the emotional attachment to the person. Tears may often fall while making nourishing meals, supervising medication, arranging transport to the doctor, etc. The feeling of having no capability to do something to make the helpless parent get better, makes things even worse. Perhaps, this is why in countries like the United States, children put their aged parents in nursing homes. They don't want to personally witness the pain that their loved ones would suffer when the illness advances.

When it's hard for the family to care for an ailing member, the responsibility falls on the caregiver. They do the feeding. They must help the patient when vomiting, and empty the urine bags. They are responsible for changing the patient's clothes, taking their temperature, and many other things most people won't dream of doing. The real challenges are not the physical needs of a patient that make the back sore and the shoulders strained, it's with their emotional needs. Caregivers admit that they have to provide enormous emotional care.

It is particularly challenging when the person being cared for is having a terminal or chronic illness. When the patient's condition deteriorates, the tasks become even more demanding. Caregivers, especially those who have come to love their patient already, most likely grieve over what is happening. They fear they would come to a point that they could no longer be able to meet the patient's needs, or do something careless that may shorten the patient's life. A simple choking could put the caregiver into a heart-pounding and hard to handle situation.

Anger and feeling rejected, despite all the efforts on the caregiver, will often make things unbearable for them. The seemingly growing and unfair demands made by the patient can be overwhelming. Researchers of a study published in The Journals of Gerontology did a study that showed that about one out of five caregivers feared that they may become violent. Also, it was found that more than one in twenty caregivers, actually did get violent with the patient.

Guilt that arises after the patient passes is common for a caregiver. They often feel that there was something more they could have done to make their patient more comfortable in their final days. They need to know that they have given all that they were capable of, and that their efforts were not unappreciated or unnoticed.

Chapter 11:
Suicide

Robin Williams' recent death left many of us, who didn't even know him, feeling bereft. How could he, who was loved by millions, take his own life? How could his life have been so unbearable that he had to end it? And how do we cope with the aftermath?

About 40,000 people in the U.S. commit suicide a year, making it the 10th leading cause of death in America. If one of those 40,000 is someone you love, it can be devastating. In the wake of a dear one's suicide, it can leave you thinking that you might be somehow at fault. Wondering what you could have done to prevent it. Feeling guilty for surviving, and not making him survive. Aching to know, "How could he leave me, if he loved me?" Expect a tidal wave of emotions that will sometimes come out of nowhere, or shift dramatically from one to the other. Your grief can be so overwhelming that you don't know how you can go on.

I have personally lost several close friends to suicide, and I can relate to the guilt that is left behind. Thinking to myself, "I wish I would have known how depressed he was, I would have stopped it" or, "If I had just listened and paid closer attention to the signs." We, as survivors, cannot beat ourselves up for the actions of others. It is not healthy for us, and it will not bring them back.

The following is a list of some of the feelings that the griever will experience after a suicide:

Denial

At first you may find the whole idea unbelievable and hard to accept. You reject the thought of it. But as reality sets in, and the numbness recedes, you experience a wide variety of feelings.

Anger

You may be angry with them for abandoning you. This fundamental emotion leaves you feeling robbed and violated. You are so angry that it's hard to forgive them for their actions. After all, no matter how they took their own life, it was no doubt shocking, especially if you were the one who found them. The image of them after their suicide can overshadow all the good memories you have of this person. Don't let it. Remember that this suicide is just one moment in their life, and it does not define who they were. Strive to remember the good things too.

Guilt

Often people feel guilty when a loved one commits suicide. You find yourself thinking that you could have saved them if only you loved them more. If only you had been a better friend or parent/spouse/son/daughter/sister/brother, etc. You play and replay scenes in your head where you missed clues of their upcoming demise. You consider the, "What ifs"…"If only you had intervened. If only you had done more." But the fact is, no matter how guilty you feel, you did not do this. You cannot blame yourself.

Despair

Finally, you may plunge into a state of despair. The loss you have suffered leaves you physically weak. You are besieged with helplessness and sadness. Nightmares wake you at night. Concentrating on the simplest tasks becomes impossible. You withdraw from your daily life and lose interest in your normal activities. You feel hopeless. This is when it's wise to seek help. Or even before you reach this state. It is quite normal to feel sad, and you may need help in working through your grief. It will take time, and there is no magic end to your mourning period. Every individual has a different path, and yours will be unique to you. But you don't have to go through these emotions alone.

Chapter 12:
Coping with Multiple Losses

How can someone cope with the death of more than one family member, when those deaths occur at the same time, or within a short period of time? What happens to the person who is grieving the death of a loved one, then losses a job, and has to move from their home or apartment because of financial conditions? Multiple losses occur more frequently than most people realize and they can complicate the mourning process.

To begin with, it is important to recognize that we grieve many changes in life, other than the death of a loved one. The break-up of any close relationship, divorce, incarceration, geographical relocation, children going off to college, destructive fires, workplace changes, or the loss of family heirlooms can bring a strong grief reaction. In most instances, these losses can bring a cascade of emotional responses as strong as those associated with the death of a loved one.

How can we cope with these massive changes or help someone who is experiencing more than one of these losses?

1.   Recognize that people suffering multiple losses will generally need much more time to sort out their feelings and deal with their losses. Often the intensity of grief will be stronger, and the mourner will need assistance in prioritizing their needs in dealing with each loss, one at a time.

2. Now more than ever, the person dealing with multiple losses needs trusted grief companions who will listen to the pain being experienced and expressed. Much commitment is needed from caregivers who will not reduce their contact with the mourner over time, or make comparisons of one mourner with another. Allowing grief to run it's course in the circumstances of multiple loss, is a gigantic commitment for the caregiver.

3. If you are suffering multiple losses, be patient with yourself. You cannot expect a speedy resolution of all of the changes that need to be addressed. There will be some trial and error moments, and you will have to try another avenue of approach, when one plan doesn't work. Do not rush yourself.

4. More than ever before, it is essential to take care of yourself. Self-care is an absolute priority since the energy drains from multiple loss are extremely high. Schedule a rest period daily, preferably in

nature, where birds, trees, water, and other wildlife can remind you of the importance of connections and the peace that will replenish your mind and body. And above all, walk, walk, walk.

5. Never forget: you are not being punished. Don't fall into thought traps like, "I'm getting what I deserve", or "This is what happens when you don't do the right thing." Such negative thinking only increases unnecessary suffering and distracts from facing the new life that multiple losses dictate. Remember, that type of thinking takes a major toll on your physical self as well as your emotional well-being.

6. Continually tell yourself you will get through this dark night of the soul. It is hell, and ever so painful, but you are a survivor, who will use the support and insight of others to adjust and start over. You are normal, even though it all feels so abnormal. There is nothing wrong with your feelings of being overwhelmed, anyone would be. Keep coaching yourself to persist, it will make a big difference in the time it takes to heal.

7. Feelings and thoughts change, and new ones will pop into your mind and body over the long haul. Look for ongoing support structures. They could be exceptional friends, a grief support group (many

members are dealing with multiple losses), a clergy person, or a professional grief counselor. The information you need, to deal with your particular circumstances, is out there. Half of the battle is finding the people who can provide an idea or two that you have yet to hear.

8.   Even though you are inundated with pain and anxiety, do not give up on listening to the best source of all, your own wisdom. You have it inside you right now, to know what to do. You are much more capable than you think you are.

When alone in the evening, ask yourself (or God, your Higher Power, even your deceased loved one) for insights to deal with a particular problem. Then listen ever so carefully for what thoughts or images come into your mind. You inherently know what is needed better than anyone else. The trick is to tap your inner wisdom with confidence.

Many people suffer multiple losses, and the resulting bereavement overload. Although multiple losses tend to exacerbate the length and intensity of the grief process, breaking down and prioritizing where to begin coping with so many changes (both inner and outer), is the place to start. It is excruciating and pain-filled work, yet success in adapting to multiple changes will happen gradually.

Keep your self-talk positive (we often are our own worst enemy), allow for a relapse or two, but know that you can outlast these massive changes, and get through your demanding ordeal.

Chapter 13:
When Grief Turns to Anger

Sometimes after a death, there are feelings of anger that arise from issues with the deceased, that were never resolved before their passing. Possibly, the anger could stem from the actual loss of having someone you care about being taken from you. These emotions can be overwhelming, because there is no way to ever talk to that person face to face again to give yourself the closure you desire.

Holding onto anger and resentment, especially for a prolonged period, can lead to a number of lifelong challenges. Continued anger and resentment can lead to many setbacks, difficulties, health issues, and trouble with intimacy and relationships. You have a choice. You can either continue to feel angry, hurt and resentful OR you can choose to let go of those emotions and live a happier fuller life. Joy, calm, understanding and peace are personal and optional choices. The decision is simple!

Maybe it's time to ask yourself these important questions:

Question #1: Would you rather be resentful or happy?

Few have lived without resentment of what they did or didn't do. Also, you may have bitterness about the circumstances in your life. It is common behavior to resent misfortune, especially if it is undeserved. Nevertheless, things happen and dealing with the happenings in your life with resentment is a useless and unprofitable path.

Do you want something more? It is human nature to want something more or different. Many years ago, I discovered my necessary key to personal happiness. It is to accept myself as I am and be content and live with what I have. I have continued my efforts to improve my circumstances within my own limitations and abilities. Such actions have contributed to my happiness. You are invited to give strong consideration to a similar path.

Question #2: Would you rather be angry or hale and hearty?

Sometimes continuing to express your anger instead of trying harder to understand your mourning is self-defeating. Anger, resentment, hate, blame, and rage are explosive emotions. Your grief journey may include these volatile reactions. Understand such expressions may be nothing more than protesting against what has happened in your life, like when someone you loved is taken. You cry out, you feel torn apart.

Although not recommended, you may direct your emotions at your companion, family, friends, doctors or even the person who has died. For some, anger, hate, blame and resentment are normal and necessary feelings. When you are raging, the intensity of your emotions may upset others, even yourself. Anger won't bring back your old life, the way it was before this loss happened. Others, as well as you, may try to over-simplify your explosive emotions. Underneath your emotions, almost always, are feelings of fear, hurt, helplessness, frustration and pain. Realize you can never go around your grief. You can't go over it or under it. You must go through it.

Listen very carefully to your explosive emotions. You may very well discover and recognize underlying feelings of pain, fear, hurt and helplessness. This understanding can lead to ways you can diminish your fiery feelings. Being hale and robust is a more healthy choice, and a personal goal for you to seek.

Question #3: Would you rather continue feeling hurt and angry or have pleasant, loving relations?

If explosive emotions are part of your journey through your grief, there are only two methods to engage in your efforts to heal. You can turn your anger emotions inward and keeping them bottled up. This does not help you heal. Bottled feelings can lead to depression, low self-esteem and thoughts of suicidal behavior. Know that your explosive emotions can be expressed, but controlled, so that you do not harm others who may help you begin a healing journey. Finding someone who will help you understand the feelings you are manifesting is important. Finding a supportive listener who will tolerate your explosive emotions without judging you, should be considered. Keep telling yourself your expressed emotions are symptoms of the hurt you feel.

One of the worst actions you can take, is to ignore or suppress feelings like anger, fear, or guilt. Experience your explosive and repressed feelings, and then move on.

Question #4: Would you rather continue to be sorrowful or calm and peaceful?

You can wish, hope, and pray that whatever has caused your sorrow could be reversed. The reality is it can't, and you feel powerless because of that knowledge. Perhaps you have struggled with the

"What ifs" and the "If I had only..." For you it becomes a new difficult reality to accept that you do not have the power and control of the circumstance that has encumbered your life. It is normal and natural to not have the ability to stay strong. Grief outbreaks come unannounced and without planning. Find someone to talk with who is willing to listen to your expressions about your significant sorrow, without judging or directing your feelings or actions. Sharing your grief can diminish your sadness.

Claim your personal peace. You cannot embrace all the pain of your grief at one time. Allow yourself to receive, figuratively speaking, a dose of grief pain, in small doses. This permits your grief to retreat one grieving pain, a measure at a time. This lets you to reach additional calmness and peace in your life.

Chapter 14:
Helping Children Through Grief

Grief is a very personal and unique experience. Children often struggle to make sense of their loss as they try to conceptualize that their loved one will not be returning to them. They grapple with the same feelings and emotions adults experience when a person we care about has died. One of the most difficult tasks for a grieving child, is to learn how to incorporate loss into his life, and to find a way to go on living after the person has died.

Regardless of their age, children can experience shock, denial, confusion, sadness, anger, blame, withdrawal, wishing, acceptance and healing. Children grieve differently at different ages. Keep in mind that younger children do not understand that death is final. Often, this concept does not resonate with a child until he is eight to ten years of age. Try and support a child based on his individual needs and his unique ability to comprehend the finality of death. It is not necessary to make any child believe that death is final. Understand that acquiring this information is a natural developmental process that will happen when a child is ready to accept the finality of death.

It is not unusual for sadness to convert to anger and

blame as children struggle to cope. These types of feelings can often range in intensity depending on a child's personality and coping skills. Some children may act in the same manner as before, other children may become withdrawn and want to be left alone. You may also notice that a child expresses a variety of feelings through angry or emotional outbursts. This is often an effort to release grief.

A typical response to loss for all ages is to imagine what it would be like if the death never occurred. This is a normal coping mechanism that provides a brief retreat from the pain of grief. Younger children may elaborately fantasize about how things could be different. This is a way for them to cope with their inability to control their environment or unexpected events around them.

Incorporating healing from loss often occurs at various times for children of all ages. Healing is difficult to measure but inevitably leads to peace and/or acceptance. Some children have a higher tolerance for dealing with loss. Help a child heal by encouraging him to express his feelings safely.

Infants and Toddlers: It is helpful to be consistent with regular routines and schedules as much as possible. This helps infants and toddlers expect some sense of control in unfamiliar circumstances.

Caregivers who are able to stay physically close can help a young children feel safe and loved.

Ages 3-6 years: Make sure children at this age know that they did not cause the death. Use simple terms and explanations and avoid giving more information than a child is seeking. This age will have minimal tolerance for sitting still for a lengthy explanation about what does not affect them personally.

Ages 7-9 years: Reassure children of this age that there will always be someone to care for them. Talk to a child about the reasons why people die and encourage him to ask questions.

Ages 10-12 years: This age group often thinks that death happens to other people and that it should not be happening to someone they know or love. They may become especially concerned that something may happen to the people who take care of them. Communicate openly with children in this age group by asking them if they have any questions. Encourage youngsters to express their feelings.

Teenagers: Teenagers feel invincible and often participate in reckless behaviors that challenge death. Often teenagers fantasize about death, including their own. They often think that death won't happen to them or anyone they know. In addition they often feel the need to outwardly express their grief when someone has died. They seek comfort from their friends, but still want adults to offer sympathy and inquire about how they are coping.

We all experience many different types of loss throughout our lives, some more painful than others. You have learned many different ways to help children and teens cope and continue living after someone dies. In addition to supporting them, remember that whenever possible tangible keepsakes, reminders about what the person was like and stories that involved the deceased can become precious to those left behind. Embracing the grief process gives everyone the gift of hope for tomorrow. All children and teens can benefit from adults who can help them validate, remember and commemorate their loss.

Chapter 15:
Grief During the Holidays

My son, Alex was born in December and passed away in January. His twenty-two days of life were right in the middle of the holiday season. This makes things exceptionally hard for me. Not only is there profound grief from the upcoming birth and death dates, but also the pressure to be happy and joyous for the holiday. I also have to stay strong for my daughter, to ensure that she has a good Christmas.

Every year, I purchase a special ornament in memory of my son for the Christmas tree. This makes me feel like he is still included and that I am able to give him a present in some way, by honoring and remembering him. On Christmas Eve, my husband and I write private notes to our son, and put them in his stocking that I have always hung up. At Christmas dinner, I light a candle for him as well. It is these little rituals that connect you to your loved one and make them not feel so far away and that they are still a part of your life.

The joy of the holidays makes emotions like grief and sadness much stronger and harder to cope with. The writers at the Valley of Life website, put together suggestions on how to cope with loss during Thanksgiving, Christmas, Hanukkah and other holiday times of year, based on the writings and discussions they have with members of their site. I thought this would be helpful to share, because those suffering loss will undoubtedly struggle with sadness during the holidays.

Holiday Tradition Can Change

There's no need to do every activity you used to do this time of year, if grief is still a major emotional factor in your life. If you feel like attending Christmas parties, or baking for your church pageant is too much this year, then skip it and take care of yourself. It is important to set realistic expectations for yourself on what you can successfully and happily complete. It may also be important to begin new traditions this holiday season to help begin making positive memories again.

No Shame

Don't feel ashamed of your emotions and don't let others make you feel bad for missing a party or church service. If they care for you they will respect your personal grieving process. Cry when you need to, and find time for yourself when you need to. Find ways to grieve, but don't isolate yourself from those that care most for you. The holidays bring up a wide range of emotions and it may take different things to help you work through each one.

Find Supporters
Seeking out friends and family members who care for you and understand what you're going through is another great way to make it through a difficult holiday season. An organized support group, church group, caring coworkers, or your good friends and family, can all provide the needed stability and listening ear that you need.

Try To Celebrate
Many feel they should try to forget or push aside their memories during the holidays. In reality, it is better to embrace them, both good and bad. Many of the bereaved have found comfort during the holidays by writing to their loved ones in a journal, a letter or a blog. Some others put up a decoration, play their favorite music or light a candle that reminds them of the deceased. Doing something to remind you of your loved one during the holidays is a great way to remind yourself that in some way they will always be with you.

Give Back To Others
Joining a service organization or throwing yourself into a local volunteer project is also a great way to cope with holiday grief. You can volunteer at a local shelter, retirement home, or library. If you are

able, buy a toy for a needy child or simply help an elderly person in your neighborhood clear their walkway. The joy you receive from paying it forward will lessen the pain that you are feeling in your heart.

Chapter 16:
What to Do with Their "Stuff"

Once the dust starts to settle, and you get back to your daily routine following the death of your loved one, you may start thinking about what to do with your loved one's belongings. You'll start thinking about this when you open your closet and see your late husbands suites hanging in there, or walk past your child's room and see their bed the way they left it. Eventually, you may decide that it's time to do something with your loved one's possessions. What you choose to do with them is entirely up to you and your family, but there are a few things to think about to prepare for this momentous project.

Here are 3 tips to prepare yourself to go through your departed loved one's belongings:

1. Do it When You're Ready
There's no timeline for going through your loved one's belongings. It is entirely up to you to decide if or when to do this. Some people like to see their departed loved one's belongings randomly throughout the day. It also may take you a while to feel like you can physically go through their things without breaking down. If the thought of getting rid of your loved one's possessions makes you feel sad or guilty, then you're not ready. Don't force yourself

to do something you don't want to do.

2. Invite Your Family to Help You

Once you're ready to go through your loved one's belongings, invite your family to help you with the process. You'll be surprised how many wonderful memories this activity will stir up, and the fun you could have sharing these memories as a family. You may also want to pass on some of your loved one's belongings to your family members, as this is the perfect opportunity to do so.

3. Do it on a "Good Day"

If you plan on going through your loved one's belongings during the upcoming weekend, but Saturday comes and you wake up feeling terrible, don't force it. Some days are just better than others when you're grieving, so be sure to go through your departed loved one's possessions on a day that you are in a good place. You're going to get emotional at some point during the process, but if you try to push through despite your somber mood, this activity will be even more difficult.

The most important thing to remember when you plan to go through your loved one's possessions, is to do it when you are ready. Additionally, don't feel like you have to purge your house of all of their belongings. Be sure to pick out the things that matter most to you and keep them as treasured memories of the person you love and miss so deeply.

Chapter 17:
How to Create a Memory
Garden

When we lose someone we love, it is only natural that we attempt to find ways to keep the fond memories of that person alive in our hearts and minds. One of the finest tributes is to create a memorial garden, a peaceful area where you can reflect on the memories of the departed. However, if a memorial garden is not well thought out from the very beginning, it could turn into an area that may become more of a burden, rather than a blessing. To help avoid such a dilemma, the following suggestions are offered to help contribute to the success of such a project.

Consider The Amount Of Area To Be Used For The Memorial Garden

A common mistake people make when constructing a memorial garden is initially making the area too large. While it is understandable that after the death of a loved one that we would not want to skimp on the size of the project, the fact remains that a garden will demand certain expenditures of time and money for its upkeep. Rather than have the garden be too grandiose for economical upkeep, a smaller, humbler garden may be the path to follow for the desired longevity of this memorial. On the other hand, if you are an avid gardener and wish to spend your free time in cultivating the area then a larger project might suit you well.

Position The Memorial Garden In A Secluded Area

Most of us would not want to bury our loved ones in a cemetery next to a busy highway, as such a setting would infringe upon our desire of having a peaceful area of meditation. Likewise, if at all possible, a memorial garden should be planted in a secluded area of your property to allow a tranquil area to reflect upon the memories of the departed.

Making The Memorial Garden Comfortable And Comforting

The garden should be a restful spot that reflects the personality of the departed. Ideally, it should be planted with fragrant and colorful flowers that the deceased enjoyed. A memorial bench would not only serve as a tasteful centerpiece of the garden, but also provide visitors a place to sit and relax. Another suggestion for a maintenance free and long-lasting addition to a memorial garden would be a wind chime, so that the music of the breezes could add to the tranquil setting.

Your local library, home improvement store, or a web search may prove useful in obtaining further details as to the type of plants and flowers that are best suited for your region. You may choose to add additional memorial items, such as markers or statues that will best suit the personality of your loved one.

Chapter 18:
Grief Journal or Letters

When you feel you are ready, writing to your loved one in a journal or in the form of a letter, will give you a sense of connection with them. You may want to start doing this right away, or it may take years before you can put your feelings into tangible words on paper. This healing exercise will help you work through any guilt or shame that may be unsettled with the deceased. You may not have been able to say goodbye to them, and by doing so in a letter, you are giving yourself the closure needed to continue living your own life.

You may just feel like talking to them, and telling them about the latest events going on in your life. Whatever you decide to write about is okay. Nobody else but you has to read it. It is also therapeutic to look back at your journal or letters in the future, to see how far you have come in your grief.

The following are some prompts to get you started, if you feel like you are unsure what to write about. Most of the time, once you start writing, the words will just flow, and you will end up feeling like a weight has been lifted.

<u>Prompts</u>

1. What are your feelings at this moment?

2. Is there anything left unsaid that you need to get off of your chest?

3. If you were not present when they passed away, express your last goodbye.

4. How do you plan on keeping their memory alive?

5. What are some memories of them that make you smile?

6. Do you need to forgive them or ask for forgiveness?

7. Are you regretful for anything you did or didn't do while they were alive?

8. What do you miss most about them?

9. Explain the depth of your love for them and the influence they had on your life.

10. Write about the current events in your life and what has happened since they passed.

Chapter 19:
Useful Grief Therapies

There are many methods out there that can help people cope with processing grief. Below are some of the methods that I have tried that have worked for me. I suggest any and all of the ones I talk about in this chapter, and I also encourage you to seek out others that may appeal to you as well. Do your research, and ask your counselor or other friends what methods they recommend.

EMDR

EMDR is an acronym for Eye Movement Desensitization and Reprocessing. It is a therapeutic method to help people let go of distressing memories, thoughts, and feelings associated with a traumatic event. It is especially helpful in getting over PTSD associated with grieving.

My counselor recommended this therapy while I was freshly coping with the loss of my son. I admit, that it was very emotional and draining, because I had to walk myself mentally through the entire situation and relive those earth shattering moments of his final days all over again. It was hard work, but I am glad that I did it, because it helped me get "unstuck" by reprogramming my thoughts.

Studies have shown that EMDR works extremely well for many clients, and it has a success rate that exceeds 80%. Researchers believe that EMDR changes the way our brain process information. It appears that, unlike other memories, traumatic memories are not processed properly and do not change over time. They are like a broken record or a tape loop that keeps on going over the same segment repeatedly without any change.

EMDR primarily works by using several simple exercises that engage the left and right hemispheres of the brain. These exercises are commonly called bilateral stimulation. Through bilateral stimulation that can be visual, auditory or kinesthetic- help this tape or recording of the traumatic memory to 'move on'. The bilateral stimulation allows the traumatic material to be processed like other memories and can provide relief from accompanying negative overwhelming emotions.

Some clients report that before EMDR, the traumatic memories were like videotapes with detailed sounds and sensations. After the sessions, the traumatic memories are more like a still black and white photograph. The traumatic memories seem to lose their intense emotional charge.

During a typical EMDR session, you are awake and

aware of what is going on at all times and you can stop the process at any point during the therapy. However it is useful to stay with the feelings that come up as long as you can so that you will be able to move through and 'reprocess' the memory.

EMDR is one of the seven ways to effectively program the mind and smash through any obstacles that can prevent you from moving towards a life of greater fulfillment.

MEDITATION

Meditation has been proven to be very effective in relieving grief and depression. Many people find it hard to focus and let their minds go empty. Some may find it difficult to ignore the thoughts that constantly enter their mind.

What worked the best for me, was listening to guided meditation recordings. You can find many guided meditation videos on YouTube and other websites. These will help you focus on breathing, and not on outside influences that tend to distract you. Daily practice will make it easier to relax, and live in the moment. Soon you will feel like a weight has been lifted and you will be more centered in your daily activities. You will notice that the extreme pain of your grief has lifted and every day tasks will be easier to handle.

<u>REIKI</u>

Reiki is an ancient Japanese system of healing that is becoming popular all over the world. Even though it is a very ancient system of healing, it retains a great deal of relevance in these times. The focus of this method of healing is to use life force energy to bring about equilibrium in the mind and body. Unlike modern Western medicine, this system pays attention to mental, spiritual and emotional wellbeing and not just physical health. This holistic method of healing offers you a wide range of advantages, many of which arise from its ability to rid the body of all pent up anger, grief, stress and other negative emotions.

I felt an extreme sense of relief after receiving my first Reiki session. It was actually so intense and beneficial for me, that I decided to take the required courses to become a certified Reiki Master Practitioner. I now have the knowledge and ability to use this incredible technique on others who are grieving, and I have witnessed the results first hand. After a session, you will feel a sense of relaxation and peace that will ease your mind and anxiety, so you are better apt to cope with life and the grief you are feeling.

Some of the most powerful benefits of Reiki healing therapy include:

Improved immunity

People whose immune systems do not work well will suffer from a variety of infectious diseases. They also fall prey to auto-immune disorders and allergies.

Better sleep

Reduced stress helps you sleep better, and this in turn, gives you many health advantages. You'll be able to perform better at work and in your personal life, if you get a good night's sleep.

Pain relief

Chronic pain can be managed with the use of Reiki, so that you don't rely on medications that may result in addiction.

Lower blood pressure

People suffering from high blood pressure issues, can use Reiki to bring their blood pressure to a normal level, due to to it's ability to reduce stress.

Better recovery from injuries or surgery

Reiki improves the body's ability to heal itself. If you have recently had surgery or chemotherapy, then you should definitely benefit from this healing system.

Increased vitality and youth
Reiki, helps the body get rid of toxins. It also improves blood circulation, thereby taking nutrients to your cells in different parts of your body.

Reiki is without doubt a very useful therapy and it can come to the aid of people of all ages and walks of life. There are many people who offer to treat people using this healing system, but the best practitioners are the ones who take the time to understand all of your problems before suggesting a solution. You will also need to invest quality time with your Reiki practitioner in order to make the most of it.

<u>AROMATHERAPY</u>
Aromatherapy helps the body heal using essential oils. There are hundreds of different types of essential oils, which are derived from plants. Each of these oils have specific properties, and certain oils will aid in relieving grief and sorrow. The essential oils that will help with grief are Roman Chamomile, Bergamot, Juniper and Lavender.

Mix several drops of these oils with a carrier oil, such as grape seed oil, and have someone give you a massage with it. You can also massage your feet, legs, arms and hands yourself if you don't have anyone readily available to do the massage for you. These oils can also be used in a diffuser, that will disperse the fragrance throughout the room.

Roman Chamomile: An anti-inflammatory, antispasmodic, and detoxifier. It will help you relax, sleep, reduce anxiety, and relieve restlessness during your grief. It will also help you to stabilize your emotions and let go of your anger. You can breathe in roman chamomile directly or with a diffuser, or used on your skin when mixed with a carrier oil.

Bergamot: Will help you with grief, because it is an anti-depressant and will balance your hormones. It's citrus fragrance alone, will lighten your mood. It can be diffused or inhaled directly, but do **not** put it on your skin. It is phototoxic to the skin, so any skin that will see sunlight within 36 hours after applying, should not have bergamot rubbed on it.

Juniper: Will help you feel love, peace, and good health during your sorrow. This oil detoxifies, regulates circulation in the kidneys, and has cleansing properties. Juniper can be inhaled, diffused, or massaged onto the skin when mixed with a carrier oil.

Lavender: A versatile oil. It will help you in your grief by allowing you to relax, reduce nervous tension, sleep, concentrate, and have mental acuity. Lavender can be inhaled, diffused, or massaged onto the skin with a carrier oil.

* In addition to using individual oils, you can also combine oils for multiple effects.

GRATITUDE JOURNAL

Find a pretty journal or notebook, and every night before you go to bed, write down things you feel grateful for in your life, no matter how big or small. You will notice that your life isn't as bad as you have imagined it to be. Even though you are suffering a great loss, there are still things around you that can bring joy to your life. It may be something as small as a smile from a stranger, a phone call from a friend, or snuggling with your favorite pet. These little things can add up, and by acknowledging them, you will condition yourself to continue to pay attention to the small joys in life, and not so much on the sadness that has been consuming you.

Chapter 20:
Journeys of Grief

On the next several pages, you will read stories of grief from various people from different walks of life, who are grieving from different circumstances. I gave each of these people a questionnaire, which asked them to discuss the different topics of grief that they have experienced, the ways they have coped, and how they keep the memory of their loved one alive.

It is my hope that these stories will resonate with a part of you, and help you through your own journey of grief.

<u>Carol's Journey of Grief</u>

I lost my mother to Altzheimer's in 2005, and my husband to a heart attack nine months later. I was fifty years old. They say it takes the second loss to grieve the first. Truth prevailed.

It's the small things that become giant in nature. When you start a conversation over the sink, and turn back to realize there is no one to reply. A song on the radio when you drive at night, the smell of gingerbread in the oven, or the need to grab the remote when you find a romantic comedy, all trigger the nerves still near the surface.

I remember watching my mother become angry and bitter when my father was taken from her. Little did I realize it was to be a teaching tool for my own survival.

Over sushi, by chance, I met Eli, my bestie now of eight years. We both lost our spouses within months. And grabbed the life raft of friendship. We talked, and talked, and cried, and mourned, and, we healed.

Another moment of fate, was an encounter last year, of a friend, Connie, whose love for poetry was contagious. Out of the clear blue sky, my pen lifted, and so did my grief. I have been writing about my life, my heart and my loss. What a cathartic experience.

Every door offers you something. Accepting the changes required, acknowledgments of your gifts of the past, and keeping your eyes looking forward, will bring you to a new path. Answer the knock, take a deep breath, and know your future depends on you.

Never Going Home

A slight little china doll, Billie is 90.
a product of life's frailties.
Broken, but not forgotten.
The world passes like the speed of light,
but she peers out the window
as if time has stopped.
Rain taps on the rooftop
The twinkle in her eyes dim slightly.

She leans forward, her fragile hands
each gracefully folded over the other.
Lips pursed, a quick sigh,
shoulders rise up and back,
as her breath gently retreats
The hazel eyes meet yours
An air of resignation,
this is her September song.
But, in a flash she returns,
Her glance slides back to those
aside who hold her dear,
tipping her head slightly.
The love wells up, she smiles
a snapshot of mere perfection.
There is never a way to say goodbye,
Just thank you, Billie is 90.

Carol Estes © 2014 www.malldog.com

<u>Payton's Journey of Grief</u>

Coping isn't easy. Grieving is hard. Getting over it? Impossible.

Growing up, I was very close with my Uncle Jamey. He would regularly ask me to come over for a game night, where we would play board games, watch movies, and laugh. The thing that made me love him the most was that special ability to make me laugh. Aside from his talent to make me laugh, he had many more qualities that made him extremely special, not only to me, but to the whole community.

Uncle Jamey was, without a doubt, adventurous. I have never known a man to have a story for everything, and these stories were sure to keep you entertained. He would walk down to my parents' house occasionally, with a pink cooler in hand. Although I knew that the cooler was originally red, and had faded to pink, it was still a guarantee that I would be giving him a hard time for having a pink cooler. We always claimed that his cooler was bottomless, because it seemed like it was impossible for it to run out of ice cold beer.

We would sit around the fire until the early hours of the morning sharing stories, listening to music, and waiting to hear the birds start chirping. He would always ask me about school, my friends, and boys. Even though he didn't know any of them, and probably didn't care, he always listened to me with such understanding. I was always flabbergasted by his knowledge of music. I swear he knew every genre, every decade. These were the nights that I lived for.

We are from a village of less than 200 people. Because of the lack of population, there wasn't ever much to do. In 1992, Uncle Jamey started a wiffleball tournament in our little town. It started small, but that has certainly changed. Every third weekend in August, our town has our annual 'Homecoming'. You would think I was lying if I even began to explain how much that wiffleball tournament has transformed. This event brings over a thousand people to our tiny metropolis. It is a two day tournament that has 16 teams, announcers, a beverage garden, fireworks, and so much more. I get to enjoy this every year, all because he had a dream.

I lost my Uncle Jamey in May of 2010 by his own hand. When I first heard the news, I dropped to my knees, just like you would see on television. No way. He wouldn't do that. The next week or two of my life was a nasty haze. I was living in my own little world of unrealities. Eventually it hit me, like I was driving my car into a brick wall with no brakes. How could I survive without him? How could I go on not being able to call him, text him, or even visit him? I had never lost anybody in my entire life, and to get him ripped from me like that made my world collapse. Naturally, I had a sense of blame. A million questions swarmed through my head every second of every day. Why wasn't I there for him? What could I have done differently? Quickly, I learned that those thoughts will consume you and control you. I just couldn't shake off the feeling that I could have done something to prevent this situation.

I learned that I was incapable of understanding the situation. I tried praying, asking, yelling, searching. I just couldn't understand. I went through a roller coaster of emotions. I would have happy days, angry days, sad days, and days where I couldn't even imagine getting out of bed.

It changed my life in a way that I will never be able to fully explain. One morning I woke up and had a serious talk with myself. I had changed. I had become dark, and sad. That wasn't me, and he wouldn't have wanted me to be so impacted. I had to understand that no matter how much I bargain, pray, dream, wish, want; he wasn't coming back. Am I going to live the rest of my life irritated, sullen, and cross? I simply couldn't. In fact, I really couldn't stand myself anymore. All I begged for was a sign from him. All I wanted was for the sunshine to come out in the morning.

Much to my amazement, the sun came up the next morning, and the morning after that, and the morning after that. As much as I thought that moving on and moving forward was impossible, I was always seeing signs. These were signs that I could survive. They were signs that he was still here with me.

Shortly after Uncle Jamey died; he sent me a pretty big surprise. I was having my graduation party at my parents' house and there were hundreds of people there. Right in the middle of the chaos of meeting, greeting, and thanking; a beautiful, breathtaking white dove swooped down and stole the show. At first, I thought it was nice, but could have been coincidental. Much to my surprise, it grew to be much bigger than that. This dove hung around for the remainder of the party, plunging down extremely close to us and doing 'tricks' over the pond. At that point, the party was on the back burner. All I could think to do was look up at the stunning, sunshiny day and thank him for coming to my party. This exquisite dove made an appearance several weeks later, just when I needed a little pick me up.

Several months later I had my first dream of Uncle Jamey since his death. I simply cannot deny that at first, I was petrified. In my dream I knew he was dead, but there was a feeling of guilt, like I wasn't supposed to be able to talk to him. However, I had to take this opportunity to ask questions. He told me that he was okay, and that we were all going to be fine. I told him how much he was missed and how much I loved him. Regrettably, I never said 'I love you' to him often while he was still with us. That was something that I took for granted, and certainly wish that I didn't. I have had several dreams of him since his death. Thankfully, each dream was very pleasant, and he always had a way of showing me that he was okay, even in dreams where no words were exchanged. He was always wearing that crooked grin. When I would wake up from these dreams, I would be sad. I wished that I could have had longer to visit with him.

These dreams often left me wishing that I could pack a suitcase and go visit him for a week or two. However, there was always a beautiful sense of relief when I would wake up knowing that he had chosen to come visit me and let me know that he was doing well. To this day, years later, he still leaves me signs. On especially rotten days, I will flip on the radio. There will be a song that I know Uncle Jamey called in and requested. It would be something that only I would understand at that exact moment.

At his funeral we had many peers and friends send us lovely gifts, wreaths, remembrance stones. I didn't want them. I didn't want a shrine of him. I didn't need to be reminded in every room of my house that he was gone. I didn't need to be reminded that I miss him more than I could ever put into words. Nevertheless, I do have a picture of the two of us sitting flawlessly beside that famous pink cooler.

There is no textbook way to grieve the death of a loved one. There is no way that your life will ever be the same. You will go through dark, miserable days. Luckily for all of us, the sun will come out tomorrow. Each day is a fresh start to wake up and conquer. Life will never be the same, but it does get easier. You will be happy again. It will be a different, unique happy. For a very long time I prayed that I would just find a little peace. It didn't come right away, in fact I gave up on the idea several times. Nevertheless, peace found its way into my life, and my heart.

On Uncle Jamey's birthday, I 'share' a beer with

him. He still frequents my dreams. He still stops to visit. I look at that pink cooler every day. Nothing makes it easier, but his little reminders surely help.

Suicide is heartbreaking. I would do anything possible to bring my Uncle Jamey back. Knowing that this isn't possible, I live every day in hopes that I can keep someone else from ending their life. If you or someone you love is in crisis, never hesitate to get help. Go to a support group, call a hotline, and reach out! If needed, I would get on the next plane to get to you. To hold you, listen, or just be. There is help available.

<u>Bonnie's Journey of Grief</u>

I lost my step dad Jim, in September 2007. He had been my step father for over 24 years. He was a funny guy who always kept us laughing. I couldn't have asked for a better step father, and we were very close.

He had open heart surgery in October 2005. After that, things went down hill very quickly. He ended up having a total of five open heart surgeries within a few months, because things just kept going wrong. After all of that, he got a serious infection. He fought that infection for two years, until it finally claimed his life in 2007.

The night he passed was a blur. I went home with my mom and sat with her for awhile. I could picture Jim sitting in his favorite spot in front of the TV, yelling at the Chicago Bears or Cubs. The house felt weird and empty without him. Even though he had been in the hospital, nursing homes, and hospice for a long time. It all just felt different now that I knew he wasn't coming back.

Those first days after he died I felt so numb and disconnected. All I kept thinking was how much I wanted him back. I didn't like the idea of what our lives would be like without him. After the funeral, and about a week or so later, I would routinely lock myself in the bathroom and cry. I'm not one to be open with my emotions. I remember thinking that the pain was never going to end. That part lasted for several weeks.

After that time, I decided that I couldn't keep being a big mush pile multiple times day and night. So I told myself that from now on, I could have one hour a day to cry my eyes out, and after that I had to stop. Then I had to pull myself together like he would want me to. Anytime that I felt like crying, I reminded myself I only got to do that once a day. I know it sounds weird, but it was the only way to keep myself from crying the whole day. It was strangely comforting giving myself permission to fall apart, but then forcing myself to end it after an hour. It wasn't always easy, but it helped me to manage my grief.

I didn't attend any support groups. I did have a few close friends that helped me to get through. I also looked up grieving online to try and understand it better. I believe it was about a year before the grief started to ease up. I noticed that I was starting to think about him and not cry. I could laugh at memories that I had of him instead of falling apart. I could look at his picture and not burst into tears. Each year it seems to get a little less painful. I visited his grave often in the beginning to feel closer to him. I can't believe that he has been gone for seven years now. I still miss him like crazy.

One thing that I do in remembrance of him, is I light a candle every Thanksgiving and Christmas. I use a glass votive candle holder that I put a label on that says "In loving memory of Jim." I always want to acknowledge the fact that someone very important is no longer there with us. That candle is a reminder that he is loved, missed and not forgotten. We also had a memory brick placed at the Hospice Center; and we do the hospice walk every year in his memory. The kids and I decorated T-shirts with his name and things he liked for the walk. It helps to be with so many others that have also lost a loved one and to see all the love for those who have passed.

The advice that I would give someone who is grieving is to allow yourself to feel that grief as unpleasant as it is. But to also remember that your loved one doesn't want you to be miserable. They would want you to continue living your life. Take it day by day, and know that even though it may not feel like it now, the pain will lessen in time. Don't be afraid to reach out to others for support and to talk about your grief and loss. Losing a loved one is the worst feeling in the world. Unfortunately, none of us can escape that. We have to keep putting one foot in front of the other and moving forward. We need to remember that our loved ones want us to do that. They want us to heal and live our lives until we meet up with them again.

I also lost my dad in April 2013. The grief from that loss is still fresh. His death was a shock to me. I will never forget the hysterical phone call from my sister telling me that he had a terrible accident. His renter had called her and told her what happened. We both live out of state so we had to frantically try to find the quickest flight out.

He lived in Florida, and had been cutting down a palm tree in his front yard in February 2013. Somehow that tree landed on him. It landed on the back of his head and smashed him into the coral rock beneath it. The amazing thing is that he actually survived that part. Not only did he survive it, but after a week or so in a coma, he woke up. He remembered us and smiled. My sister and I were beyond relieved. He had done what the doctors said he couldn't.

We made multiple trips back and forth to Florida, juggling families and our dad. We left on the day they were taking him off the ventilator, and he was supposed to be getting moved to a rehabilitation center. We had a family friend check on him almost every day while we were gone, to let us know how he was doing. We had planned on going back as soon as we could. Before we were able to return, my sister got a frantic call from the friend, telling us something had happened to our dad. No one from the hospital had bothered to call us. We had only been gone for a little over a week and he had taken a major turn for the worse. We went back to Florida and could not believe our eyes. He looked horrible, I couldn't understand what had happened in that short period of time. He died about a week or so after we arrived, from pneumonia and sepsis. An infection had taken another one of my loved ones.

I was beyond shocked, and I was wracked with guilt. I kept thinking I never should have left him. He had only been gone for about ten minutes before the hospital was telling us that we had to make arrangements to get him out of there. They put me on the phone with funeral homes. I was still trying to digest that he was gone, and they were pushing me to make decisions. It was horrible. I went back to his house that night, and I felt like I was going to be sick. I sat on his couch and cried and cried. I kept looking at all of his stuff and how he had left it. It was so hard to believe that he was never going to walk back in his house again. I was thinking how he had got up the day of the accident not knowing that day was going to be the beginning of the end. He had got up and had coffee, paid his bills, and checked his stocks. Then he went out to cut down that tree. He never went in his house again.

We made arrangements as quick as we could and decided to bury him in the Veteran's Cemetery. The day before the funeral, my sister and I had to pick out his clothes to bury him in. My dad was a Harley guy. He always wore a T-shirt, jeans, and his leather Harley vest. That is what we chose for him. I was alone that night and the clothes were laid out on the bed. I stood there looking at them and started bawling. He should be in those clothes and alive. I laid on the bed with the clothes and just cried my eyes out. He always had handkerchiefs in his pocket too, so I took one of his red handkerchiefs and wiped my tears with it. Then I put it in his vest pocket. I thought now my tears are in his pocket for eternity. It makes me cry just remembering it. The pain was so intense and raw and almost unbearable.

I was having a really rough time accepting that he was gone. I was an emotional wreck, although no one but me knew that. One night a couple of weeks after he passed, I had a dream about him. In the dream he said to me, "There is a difference between the living and the dead. You have to decide if you want to be with the living or the dead." He said this is his stern tone he used a lot. I knew that came from my dad. It sounded just like something he would say. He was telling me to knock it off and to focus on the living. That's exactly something he would say to me.

That one dream helped me to deal with my grief. It reminded me that he did not want me so upset, and that he was watching me. I knew I had to start pulling myself together and take his advice. I still cry over his death. Little things will set it off. Then I remember his words and try to focus on the loved ones that are still here. I know that when I think of him, he doesn't want me to be sad. He doesn't want me to focus on his death, but to remember how he was when he was alive.

His first great grandchild was born one week after he passed. My dad had been looking forward to that moment. It still upsets me that he missed it. Having Tristan though, has also helped with the grief. I know my dad wants me to enjoy him and to make sure that Tristan will know who he was.

Having gone through the loss of my step-dad as well, I know that this pain will continue to ease in time. I will always have days that are going to be hard, and I will continue to miss him everyday. I think he taught me in that dream to remember how fragile life is, and how quickly someone can be gone without ever getting to say goodbye. He always ended his conversations on the phone with "I love you." So that is something else I have to ease my pain. The last words that we spoke to each other were "I love you." Even though he had woke up from his coma, he never had the opportunity to speak again due to the ventilator.

Facing each day after losing a loved one is difficult; time does help lessen that pain. During the beginning stages it feels like you will never laugh again or be happy. Doing things in remembrance of your loved one helps diminish the pain somewhat. In his memory I do the same thing with the candle that I did for my step-dad. It is lit every Thanksgiving and Christmas. I keep his picture next to my bed and like to think that he is watching over me. My sister and I are also going to have a memorial brick placed in the Veterans Memorial for him.

Grieving is painful, there is no way around it. There is also no right or wrong way. You just have to get through it the best that you can. Don't be afraid to reach out for support. Don't let anyone tell you how much time you should grieve. Know that you are going to be okay, and that you will get through this. You may not believe that for awhile, but it's true. We all have our unique ways to get through it. By sharing our stories, we may somehow help someone else going through it.

I believe in God, so I believe that we will be reunited with all of our loved ones who left before us. If that is your belief as well, then hold on to that and let your faith sustain you. My heart breaks for everyone who is grieving the loss of someone they love. I pray that you find peace and comfort.

Leslie's Journey of Grief

My Grandmother Alyce was someone that was there for my family in a way that I never realized until her passing. So many things that someone does for you that you do not appreciate fully until they are gone. My family had many hardships growing up, but my Grandmother helped many times, to where my little brother and I didn't really notice, because the help went on behind the scenes. She gave money to my mother who was at times too proud to take it, so my Grandmother would have her do work for her.

My Grandmother even had me work for her at times. I remember rubbing her feet for 30 minutes because she told me she would give me a dollar for every minute of the massage! When I was young, I wanted a diamond ring so badly. I had seen one at a local jeweler, and it was $100.00. It had a little speck of a diamond, but I didn't care! My Grandmother had me do things for her every week and would give me money so that I could eventually get my ring.

My little brother and I would get so excited when my Grandmother would come over. She would usually make a huge pot of her famous spaghetti or our favorite chicken noodle soup. We would laugh with joy when we would help her unload all the groceries. She would go shopping for the items she needed to cook, and for much more than that. We always thought she was just so silly and couldn't help herself and bought more, when really she was helping our family out, by buying the food we couldn't afford. She would say, "Oh gosh, I know I shouldn't go to the store hungry! I bought so much extra stuff! Oh, these hamburgers looked so good, and so did these apples! Oh wow… yep, I thought all this cereal looked so good, I couldn't pick just one. While I was there, I saw these cookies and couldn't help myself."

We would get so happy and tell my mom, "Grammy Alyce really knows how to shop, mom!!" When my mom went shopping, our trips barely contained cookies or junk cereal. My mom bought what we needed and what she felt was healthy.

Whenever she would visit, we would run to the car barefoot and in pajamas, to do a Dairy Queen run after dinner. My Grandmother would insist that we needed dessert before bed. I remember as a kid shaking so hard because I could never make up my mind of what dessert I could get, because my Grandmother would tell me that I could get anything I wanted!

My Grandmother loved her sweets but sadly that

was one of her biggest struggles. She was a heavier lady but she was so beautiful, and just really had this killer smile and infectious laugh. She was diabetic and didn't let that curb her love for candies. Even when she passed away, we found boxes of her hidden Fannie May chocolate stash everywhere.

My Grandmother passed away 22 years ago, and I will never forget that day, because I was with her. I feel fortunate to have spent the last day on earth with her, but at the same time it was scary for me at sixteen, to handle the situation. My Grandmother called earlier in the day, and asked if I wanted to go golfing with her and her cousin. I was not going to go, but there was something in my mind that told me I didn't really get to spend that much time with her anymore, so I should do it!

We had played about three holes of golf, and she started getting cramping in her arm and her chest hurt. She got very tired, so we decided to stop and go out for dinner. We ate at one of the local places, and she ordered a very diabetic friendly meal. It was her new life since after the angioplasty, she had dropped about five pant sizes working very hard on losing weight. We talked politics and who she would vote for in the upcoming election, which was not Clinton of course since she was a die-hard republican. She bragged to her cousin about how I was so talented, and since she didn't brag right in front of me that much, I was really excited. After dinner she paid the check and let me keep the change, and said I could split it with my brother.

It was the ride home that really changed everything. I was sitting in the back seat, and my Grandmother was driving. She got sick all of a sudden, so her cousin had her pull over so she could drive. She kept saying how she needed to use the bathroom so we were in a hurry to get to my house. Sadly we never made it there as she started making these strange noises and then started turning colors. I remember crying and screaming because I didn't understand what was happening, but her cousin did. Her cousin who was in the car, was a nurse. She pulled the car over, and had me run to a neighbor and asked them to call the ambulance, because my Grandmother was having a heart attack. She started CPR until the medics go there, and loaded my Grandmother in the ambulance. We had also called my mother, who arrived and went into the ambulance with her. Then my Grandmother's cousin took me home.

After the ambulance came, there was a waiting period where I was at home and felt that everything was going to be okay. I was sixteen years old, and felt she was too young to die. she was 68. I just assumed we would get a call saying that they got to the hospital, that she was in a room, and we could see her tomorrow.

An hour or so after I got home, my mother called the house and wanted to speak to my dad. I was very angry because she wouldn't tell me if my Grandmother was okay. When my dad got off the phone he said, "Kids, your Grandmother died." and I blew up. He wanted to hug us, but I ran screaming into my bedroom very angry that he told me that, and that he said it in that way that was so blunt. No, "I'm very sorry…", but honestly, how do you tell someone that their loved one has passed on?

I went into my room, locked the door and wouldn't come out or talk to anyone, because I wanted time to stand still. I even insisted that I was "fine" and went to school the next day. I wanted to pretend none of it happened, and also had so much guilt wondering that maybe we should have went to the hospital when my Grandmother said her arm was cramping. I felt like it was my entire fault and the scene kept playing over and over in my head.

My friends at school didn't have too much to say except for a good ol', "That sucks dude, I am sorry", but they were young too, and their grandparents were either living or died when they were really young. I think I insisted on going to school that day because of a few things. Having that routine and something else to focus on, other than the scene stuck on repeat. I thought that I would be surrounded by my friends and that they would be supportive, lending a shoulder to cry on, but that never happened.

I ended up going through the school day lost in a daze, until after lunch. I went to science class and was starting to break down. It didn't help that I was really bullied by kids in that class every darn day. I finally snapped on them that day, and after that, they kind of toned down making fun of me. One kid that sat in front of me was making a scene and picking on me and I just screamed at him with a flood of curse words, very, very loudly. I let him know where he could take his snotty mouth. The teacher looked shocked and got angry with me too, but I told him basically to, "Stick it", and that I watched my grandmother die the night before. I grabbed my things and flew out of the room, up to the office and demanded that they call my mom to get me.

Sadly when I lost my Grandmother it was in the 90's and there weren't any online forums for me to explore. I am sure there were support groups but even back then my mother knew nothing about them. My mom clung to the church and her family but I kind of pushed everyone and everything away. Things seemed to get a little better after my Grandmother's funeral. I feel that seeing her being put in the ground made it feel more final. After the funeral we all went back to her house and when we opened the door it smelled so strongly of her that I expected her to walk around a corner and say she was just kidding. We all talked about her for hours, the crazy things she did and said her silly golf swing, when she would get mad and so many other memories of her. For some reason, sitting around and just talking about her really helped. It took a long time before the feeling left. At first I was crying all day, then I was crying once a day, once a week and then once a month and so on.

I always feel the need to get Dairy Queen on the day she died, or at least around the day of her death. Actually, anytime I get a Blizzard, I kind of think of her a little. The same thing happens when I step foot into a Fannie May chocolate store. My mom tries to have a family get together around her birthday, which is usually around Labor Day since she was born on September 5, 1924. On my wedding day I took a bouquet from my wedding to my Grandparent's grave site. I cried a lot at that moment because I really wished they were there. I think that I will feel that way during any major event in my life.

I keep a small bottle of Red Door perfume in my curio cabinet and most people don't even notice it being in there. When I really miss her I will smell the bottle or even wear a little when I need to feel like she is close to me. Every time I make her "Polish Spaghetti" (because she's 'Polish' she said, "Italians are not the only ones that can make spaghetti!"), and every time I make that Chicken Noodle Soup or eat the Breakfast Treat "S" cookies from Stella D'Oro, I think of her.

I make jewelry, and most recently I have taken my jewelry making to a different level, and it was all inspired by my Grandmother. My Grandmother was Catholic and gave me a rosary for darn near every event in my life. I started making rosaries and every time I make one I think of her. I have started to bling out saint medals and other religious things, because I think of all the costume jewelry and "blingy" stuff she used to own. Making these crafts and cooking are just a few ways that I keep her memory strong, and since she loved my creativity I feel that she would be proud of me.

When you are grieving, it is easy to think of all the things that you could have done or how you should have treated that person differently. That person is gone and you will eat yourself up inside with these kinds of thoughts. Your loved one is looking at you from above, and God knows only peace. They know that you are sorry, love you, and just want you to live your best life until you can see them again. Grief is normal, but do not let what you have done or said cloud the memory of them.

I am a firm believer in having a "signature scent". Now that my Grandmother has passed away, I wear the same perfume most of the time so that people have a scent memory associated with me. Does your loved one have a certain perfume or cologne they wore? Get a bottle to keep! If not, was there a scent they really liked? Lemon? Coffee? Maybe they really liked cookies, so get a candle that smells like that. Having a scent is a powerful thing, because it can make it seem as if they are present. It is very comforting. If you can, even a shirt or a pillow from their house carries a personal scent with them. A pillow is great because you can hug it.

I know that for myself, being Polish, food is a huge part of our life. After my Grandmother passed away, I know that I ate some of her favorite foods. There was a lot of comfort in having a massive bowl of the soup she made. Granted, I cried while making it, but there was something that made me feel better by eating it.

Sometimes you need something to do when you are grieving that is also relaxing and creative. It can help cheer you up. Think of the funny things they said or did, and write them down to remember them. I think having a little book dedicated to them, even if it is just a notebook and not a scrapbook, is a wonderful thing. In the future when you miss them, you will have something amazing to look at. I know one of the things that really helped me, was listening to all the stories of the silly things my Grandmother did. Talk to your family and loved ones and get some of these stories. Sometimes a family member might bring up old fights, but just let them know that no amount of arguing will change the past. Love that family member or friend for what they did do that was positive.

<u>Linda's Journey of Grief</u>

Patti and I have been friends for over twenty years. We hit it off right from the beginning. We were both from Chicago, now living in California. We would laugh like school girls each time we were together. Patti and her husband spent their lives healing others, through their seminars and teaching of Guided Imagery. I became a therapist through their training. Patti was a cancer survivor for over thirty years. A year ago she was diagnosed with stage four pancreatic cancer. In three weeks she was gone. I miss her every day.

The day I got the phone call from her husband, I fell apart. I can't even describe the sound that came out of me. All I can remember is he said, "She went peacefully in her sleep." How could this be? It doesn't make sense she said she would beat it like she did so many years ago. Why wasn't I with her? So many questions that began with the word "Why?"

I never said goodbye. Now that I think of it, she would never say goodbye, she would say, "Namaste." One day we talked about dying. I told her I would go first because I was a year older. I promised to come back as a bird to say hello. Patti said, "I will come back as a butterfly."
I decided I would attempt to paint her portrait and

give it to her husband at her celebration of life. I remember the excitement, and when her face emerged from the canvas, I began to cry. I wanted so much to do a good job. While painting this portrait I said out loud, "Patti I need your help."

A very beautiful butterfly came to my window and fluttered it's wings. I shouted, "You kept your promise!" This butterfly would come to the window each day until her portrait was finished. It gave me the courage to go on. I would also find white feathers, and I knew she sent them.

Her daughter has kept Patti's Facebook page, and it is so comforting to see others who loved her write about their memories.

I went through most of the stages of grief. The way I am able to go on with the loss of my good friend is I know she is still around and I remember the laughter and her gentle loving nature. Once in awhile the beautiful butterfly comes into my garden and stays for awhile to say, "Hello my friend."

Below is the finished portrait of Patti:

To see more of Linda's paintings, visit:
http://www.paintingsilove.com/artist/lindamorrison

Cynde's Journey of Grief

I lost my mother in October of 2008. She was 81 years old, and had been in ill health for a number of years. When she passed over, I felt so all alone. I really didn't get a chance to say good-bye. She had experienced a major heart attack and we knew she would not recover. We took her off of life support because we knew she did not want her life prolonged if she was not going to recover. The hardest thing I ever had to do was to go to the funeral home with my father and plan her funeral, as we knew she would not make it through the next 24 hours. The feeling of loss and grief had already begun even before her actual, physical death. I knew that it was her time to leave us. Her journey here, was over and she was about to begin a new one, in spirit. I really miss her and I still talk to her when I need advice or just feeling the need to "connect" with her.

Seven months after my mother passed, my husband was facing open heart surgery for aortic valve replacement. A pretty routine surgery for the most part. Although he was nervous about it, he came through it just fine. However, a few days after returning home from the hospital, he went out for a short walk with his son and our grandson (which the Dr ordered), and on the way back to our house, he fell to the ground. Fortunately, my step-son and his wife (who is a nurse) were there, and they began working on him until the EMT's arrived.

I held his hand and rubbed his arm, telling him to hang on and told him how much I loved him. He opened his eyes and looked at me and a few seconds later, went into a seizure. I knew then that he was not going to make it. I could not believe this was happening. I felt as though I was in the midst of a bad dream. I kept saying, "This can't be happening!".

When we arrived at the hospital, they took us to a room and told us the Dr would be in to talk to us. I knew then, that my husband had passed. It was so hard to fathom why this happened. We had only been married seven years, and we both were looking forward to his retirement in a few months. It was not to be.

Five months after my husband passed, I got a phone call late on a Friday night. It woke me out of a sound sleep. It was my daughter in law's mother calling, and I couldn't understand why she would be calling me. Then my senses cleared, and I realized it had to be something bad for her to call me. She told me that my son, daughter in law, and two granddaughters had been in a bad accident earlier in the evening, and my five year old granddaughter did not make it. I just could not think, or even breathe at that moment. Death had re-visited me once again! I kept thinking, "How could this have happened? Why is this happening?"

The next morning my older son and I packed up and drove the 1200 miles to their home. My youngest son was still hospitalized, and thankfully recovering. His wife and other daughter were unhurt. We were all just moving about, going through the motions. Somehow we got thorough that time. I hated to leave to go back home but I needed to return to work. The sense of loss that I felt that year was so immense. But through it all, though I could make no real sense of it, I knew within my heart and soul that it was their time to leave this world, for whatever reason. Though we all felt the pain of loss with each passing, my faith kept me going. I knew that one day we would all meet again and what a joyous time that will be!

With each passing, my spiritual faith kicked in and I was able to keep functioning on a pretty normal level, although at times, I felt as though I was on auto-pilot. Just doing what I had to do. When my husband passed, I found it hard to sleep. My children wanted me to go to the Dr to get some sleeping pills but I refused. I had to work through this on my own. Initially, I had much support from my husband's children and his siblings. As time went on, that support pretty much disintegrated, and I only heard from his sister. His children do not bother to stay in touch. I do believe that much of this stems from anger that I was the beneficiary of his entire estate. However, I did give a generous gift to each of his children. What bothered me even more, was the fact that I had no support from my sister or father. No one bothered to call me after the funeral to see if I was doing alright. None of my cousins (who I had been close to while growing up) even bothered to acknowledge my loss. I felt totally abandoned. It has taken me a long time to get over it. At times, the pain returns but I don't dwell on it.

When my granddaughter passed, even though it was at the hands of a drunk and drugged driver, I could not find it in my heart to hate him. Neither could my son and daughter in law. We were all just so saddened that a beautiful young life had been cut short and we would never see her grow up and experience all the things that a girl should experience. Even though the man that hit them went to prison for fifteen years, there was still no hatred. We were just happy that he was off the street and could do no harm to anyone else.

It has been five years since her passing, and I still have moments of loss and tears but again, I know that there was a reason for her early passing, and that I will see her again one day. I never once exploded or blamed God for taking my loved ones. But that is just me. We all experience grief in different ways. I did not go to any support groups. Mainly because the times they were offered were during the day and I had to work. I found an online grief forum that helped me so much. The love and prayers they offered helped me more than anything else during these times of grief.

I really did not notice any certain period of time where I actually felt as though my grief was lifting. I don't think it ever goes away completely. It was a very gradual thing. I had my work to keep me occupied so that helped me immensely. But at those times when I would lie awake at night missing my husband, or at the times I would think about my granddaughter and mother the most, (their birthday, holidays, etc.) I would lapse into a short period of grief. I was always able to bring myself out of it though. Again, I attribute it to my faith.

The first couple of years after my husband died, I bought him a birthday card, anniversary card, Christmas card, etc. and expressed my feelings to him in them. I also donated money to the Wounded Warrior Program for Christmas. My husband had served many years in the military, and would have retired from it, had he lived. I send a floral arrangement to my granddaughter in care of her parents, every birthday and Christmas. Even though she is physically gone, she still is with us in spirit. We also place a special memorial poem in the local newspaper for my mother.

When I decided to landscape my front yard, I made an area for each of my loved ones and planted special plants and yard ornaments for each one. Unfortunately, I have since moved, but I brought the lawn ornaments along with me so that I can set up a memorial area for each of them.

Be easy on yourself. Grieve as long as you need to. There is not a time limit on grief. Do not listen to those who think they are helping you by telling you to "Snap out of it!" or "You should be over it by now!" They obviously have never lost a loved one and gone through the grieving process. If it becomes unbearable, seek help. Don't try to go it alone.

Chapter 21:
Tips to Help the Grieving

When suffering from grief, people often feel isolated and alone. If they choose to be alone, then you should respect that. However, do not completely avoid the subject of their loss or stay away from the griever. By interacting with them, you are demonstrating that you care about them.

The following suggestions will help guide you on interacting with someone who is going through grief:

Do not say that you understand how the person feels.
Even if you have gone through a similar experience as the person who is grieving, you cannot fully comprehend their exact situation.

Avoid cliches.
For example, do not tell the griever, "Time will heal the wounds." For some people this may be true, but for others the hurt will always be there.

Avoid telling them to be strong.
People who are dealing with grief are very vulnerable. Telling them to be strong is an unnecessary burden that they won't be able to

overcome in the beginning stages.

Look for signs of a prolonged problem.
You need to understand the grieving process. If you see signs of a long-term problem developing, then encourage them to get counseling or an evaluation from a medical professional.

Write a personal note which displays compassion and kindness.
Written words are permanent and can be a real source encouragement for the griever during the rough times ahead.

Make yourself available.
Sometimes the person who is grieving just needs you to be there to offer a listening ear or a shoulder to cry on.

Encourage the grieving person to write down their thoughts.
This is a powerful way to get the grieving person to release their emotions and not keep them bottled up. It can be a great healing process.

Ask what you can do.
Offer to do household tasks, shopping or cooking for the person while they grieve. The grief can be so strong in the beginning, that they find themselves

unable to do simple, everyday chores.

Understand the importance of the loss.
Do not trivialize the loss in conversation. Choose your words wisely, being sensitive to their feelings of loss and love for the one who has died.

Talk about your own losses and how you handled them.
By sharing your experiences, you can empathize with the person who is grieving. You are not telling them that you understand what they are going through, you are simply making the attempt to connect with them on an emotional level.

Chapter 22:
Poetry of Grief and Hope

Never Be the Same
The moment that you left me,
my heart was split in two;
one side was filled with memories;
the other side died with you.
I often lay awake at night,
when the world is fast asleep;
and take a walk down memory lane
with tears upon my check.
Remembering you is easy,
I do it everyday;
but missing you is a heartache
that never goes away.
I hold you tightly within my heart,
and there you will remain;
you see life has gone on without you,
but will never be the same.

- Author Unknown

Gone, But Not Forgotten

You can shed tears that he is gone.

Or you can smile because he has lived.

You can close your eyes and pray that he'll come back.

Or you can open your eyes and see all he's left.

Your heart can be empty because you can't see him.

Or you can be full of love you shared.

You can turn your back on tomorrow and live yesterday.

Or you can be happy for tomorrow because of yesterday.

You can remember home and only that he's gone.

Or you can cherish his memory and live on.

You can cry and close your mind, be empty and turn your back,

Or you can do what he'd want.

Smile, and open your eyes, love and go on.

Gone, but not forgotten.

- Author Unknown

Do Not Stand at My Grave and Weep

Do not stand at my grave and weep,
I am not there, I do not sleep.
I am in a thousand winds that blow,
I am the softly falling snow.
I am the gentle showers of rain,
I am the fields of ripening grain.
I am in the morning hush,
I am in the graceful rush
Of beautiful birds in circling flight,
I am the star shine of the night.
I am in the flowers that bloom,
I am in a quiet room.
I am in the birds that sing,
I am in each lovely thing.
Do not stand at my grave and cry,
I am not there. I do not die.

-by Mary Elizabeth Frye

Grief Support Links

The Compassionate Friends:
Local chapters across the USA and an online community, provides grief support, after the death of a child or sibling of any age.
http://www.compassionatefriends.org/home.aspx

SHARE:
Infant and pregnancy loss support in the USA.
http://www.nationalshare.org

Grief Share:
International grief support.
http://griefshare.org

Sisterhood of Widows:
Widow support.
http://sisterhoodofwidows.com

Grieving.com:
Forums for all areas of grief.
http://forums.grieving.com

Widow and Widower Support:
http://www.nationalwidowers.org

Pet Loss: http://www.petloss.com

Survivors of Suicide:
http://www.survivorsofsuicide.com

Alliance of Hope:

For suicide survivors.

http://www.allianceofhope.org

<u>Healing The Grief</u>

The author of this book, Lora C Mercado, has founded the website, Healing The Grief. There you will find articles, poems and links to helpful resources to those who are experiencing loss and grief.

Website: http://healingthegrief.com

Facebook:
https://www.facebook.com/healingthegrief

Twitter: https://twitter.com/HealingTheGrief

YouTube:
https://www.youtube.com/channel/UCJfFpPwAEzx jxIlUg49tBRA

Pinterest: http://www.pinterest.com/healingthe

About the Author

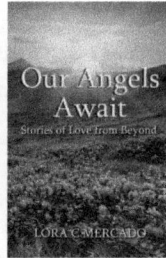

In tribute to her son's passing, Lora C Mercado has been on a quest to help bring peace to those who are in a state of grief.

Read her book "Our Angels Await, Stories of Love from Beyond", if you enjoy inspirational stories from people across the globe who have had connections with loved ones who have passed away.

Our Angels Await, Stories of Love From Beyond
http://www.amazon.com/dp/B00FIV93OA

Lora Mercado is also a Usui Reiki Master Practitioner and ordained minister, who has married over 100 couples.

To contact Lora, please send an email to: MargueritePublishing@gmail.com

Be sure to check out these other titles by Lora C Mercado:

SPIRITUAL:
Our Angels Await, Stories of Love from Beyond
http://www.amazon.com/dp/B00FIV93OA

POETRY:
Reflections Within, A Free Verse Poetry Collection
http://www.amazon.com/dp/B00LNDX71M

COOKBOOKS:
Oh Cheese! Homestyle Cheesy Favorites
http://www.amazon.com/dp/B00J3Y77TG

Tasteful Memories, A Collection of Family Comfort Food Recipes
http://www.amazon.com/dp/B00IPMF64K

Gimme That Chocolate! A PMS Survival Cookbook
http://www.amazon.com/dp/B00IT63L8U

The Garden Digest, Fruit and Vegetable Recipes for Health and Weight Loss
http://www.amazon.com/dp/B00M7BBFP4

Bunch O' Brunch
http://www.amazon.com/dp/B00JGYBV3Q

A Bundle of YUM!
http://www.amazon.com/dp/B00JLLY74Y

PUBLISHING:

YOU Can Self Publish!
Tips, Tricks and Valuable Resources
http://www.amazon.com/dp/B00MU0O9DC

CHILDREN'S BOOKS:

1, 2, 3 Count with Me: An Early Learning Counting Book
http://www.amazon.com/dp/B00LV2PVMS

Black Cats: Fun Facts and Myths
http://www.amazon.com/dp/B00MI91P6E

NOTES: